PAGE PUBLISHING
Conneaut Lake, PA

First originally published by Page Publishing 2024

ISBN 979-8-89315-559-4 (pbk)
ISBN 979-8-89315-560-0 (digital)

Printed in the United States of America

Charlie
THE G.O.A.T.

MARY FILSHIE

Illustrated by Ray Mota

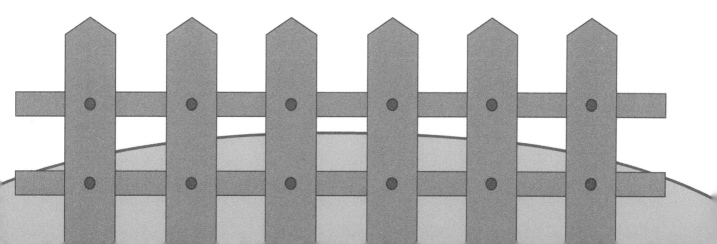

One spring day, Rancher Helen called her good friend Farmer Mary and said, "I have a baby goat that needs a family. Can you help me?"

The Farmer family said, "Yes, of course!"

When the Farmer family got to the baby goat, she was very tiny and very scared. They took the baby goat home.

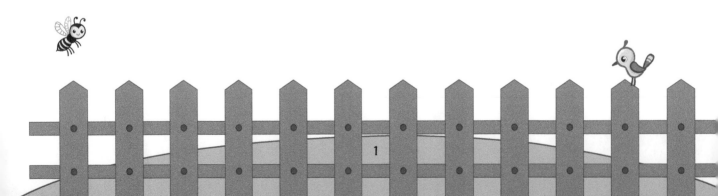

All night long, the Farmer family kept watch and fed the little goat tiny drops of goat's milk with a bottle.

To the Farmer family's surprise, the next
morning the baby goat looked up and asked
in a teeny tiny voice, "Are you my mom?"
Farmer Mary hugged the baby goat
tight and said, "Yes, I am."

Over the next few weeks, the baby goat went everywhere with the Farmer family. If they ran errands, she went with them. If they went to work in the big city, she went with them.
Every day, she got stronger and stronger.
Every day she knew nothing but love.
The Farmer family loved the little goat so much!

Finally, it was time for the little goat to
meet all the other farm animals!
She sniffed the horses, she ran with the
cows, and she slept with the pigs. It was
a fun day! She loved the farm.
When she came in the farmhouse that night
she said, "Can I please have a name?"
Farmer Mary remembered a sweet little girl who was
helping at Rancher Helen's. Her name was Charlotte.
Farmer Mary said, "How about we call you Charlie?"

Charlie went out the next day and told all the farm animals she had a name, and it was Charlie! The farm animals only picked on her. "Your ears are too long. Your horns are crooked. Your legs are bowed." Charlie was so sad. She ran into the farmhouse and told the Farmer family what the other animals said and how it made her feel small, tiny, and weak. Farmer Mary held Charlie tight and said, "Charlie, each of us is special and unique. The world would be boring if we were all made exactly alike."

At her first vet appointment, the doctor
said to the Farmer family that Charlie's
bowed legs needed to be fixed.
They would have to splint her legs and wrap them
with special tape to straighten them. Charlie
would have to wear the splints for months!

Charlie took a few steps and realized she could still
run and jump even with splints on! She went out
to show the other farm animals her new splints.
They all laughed at her. She was very sad.
For several weeks, she wore the splints. For several
weeks, she was picked on. The biggest bully was Lenny
the Lamb. He always called her "Crooked Legs Charlie."

Charlie was by herself one day under the willow tree when in the distance she heard a voice. "Help me!" she heard. She followed the voice to a big hole and found Lenny the Lamb stuck at the bottom of the hole. "Go get help, Charlie. I'm stuck in here, and it's getting dark out!"

"I have an idea that might work, Lenny," Charlie said.
Lenny grumbled, "Just go get help, Charlie! Go
find someone who will know what to do."

Charlie ran to find the herd. They all stood around, and no one had any idea how to help Lenny.

Finally, with her brave little voice, Charlie said, "Here, use these to help save Lenny." She began to bite at her special wraps that held her splints together. "Put the wraps over my horns, throw them into the hole, and we can pull Lenny up!" Mr. Horse threw the wraps down the hole and Lenny grabbed them. Charlie backed up and pulled Lenny out of the hole! Everyone cheered!

Everyone cheered except Lenny the lamb. Confused he asked, "Charlie, I've picked on you and made fun of you for weeks. Why did you help me out of the hole?"

"Because each of us is special and unique. This world would be pretty boring if we were all alike," Charlie said.

Charlie and Lenny hugged. Charlie, for the first time, felt like a part of the herd!

"Charlie, look!" yelled Nessie the rabbit. "Your legs are straight! The special splints worked! Now, you're just like the rest of us!"

Charlie smiled. "Actually, I kind of like being a little different. That's what makes me Charlie. There's not another goat exactly like me."

About the Author

Mary lives in Sonoma County, California, with her husband. They share the duties of running a small farm with many animals.

Ray Mota, the illustrator, is a friend of the Filshie family. He loves the farm and the animals. There was no one better to bring Charlie to life on paper!

Printed in the USA
CPSIA information can be obtained
at www.ICGtesting.com
CBHW040912011124
16733CB00036B/1313